מִצְווֹת

MITZVOT are commandments.

There are two kinds of MITZVOT.
Some are called
MITZVOT BEN ADAM LAMAKOM.
These commandments tell us how
we should behave toward God.

In this book you will learn about
the other MITZVOT-
MITZVOT BEN ADAM LECHAVERO.
These commandments help us to
know right from wrong. They teach
us how to behave with other people.

When we do a Mitzvah, we fulfill
God's commandment.

MITZVOT help us to live a good life. You are going to learn about MITZVOT that you can do. You are now ready to begin your journey to a good life. Make this astronaut you. Draw in your own face. Write your name on the spaceship. Can you write your name in Hebrew? If so, write that on the spaceship, too.

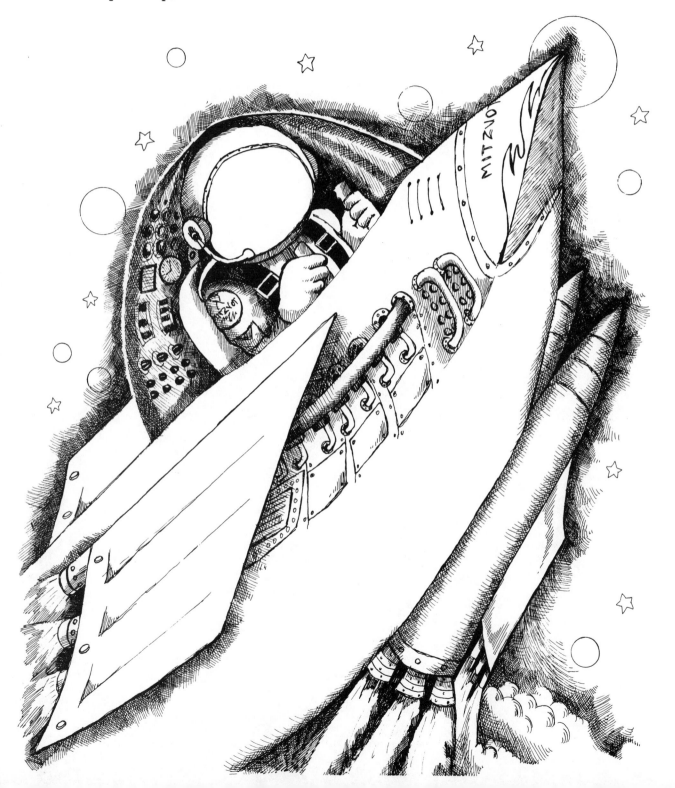

You honor your parents when you love and respect them. It is a Mitzvah to honor your father and your mother. This Mitzvah is called KIBBUD AV VA-EM. Here is a special way of showing KIBBUD AV VA-EM. Color in the award and cut it out. Then give the award to your parents.

There are many ways to honor your parents. Here are 4 ways to KIBBUD AV VA-EM. Choose one that you will do. Color that picture and cut it out. Then paste it in the gift box on the next page.

Paste your Mitzvah picture in the gift box. Color the box and the ribbon. Then give it to your parents. Be sure to remember to do the Mitzvah of KIBBUD AV VA-EM.

SHALOM means peace. BAYIT means house. SHALOM BAYIT is a Mitzvah and it means peace in the home. But SHALOM BAYIT means more than not fighting at home. You have SHALOM BAYIT when members of your family love and help one another. Make a record of the things you do to keep SHALOM BAYIT. Use the stickers on the next page to mark the chart each time you keep SHALOM BAYIT.

Color the stickers. Cut them out and paste them on the SHALOM BAYIT chart
to record each thing you did to follow this important Mitzvah.

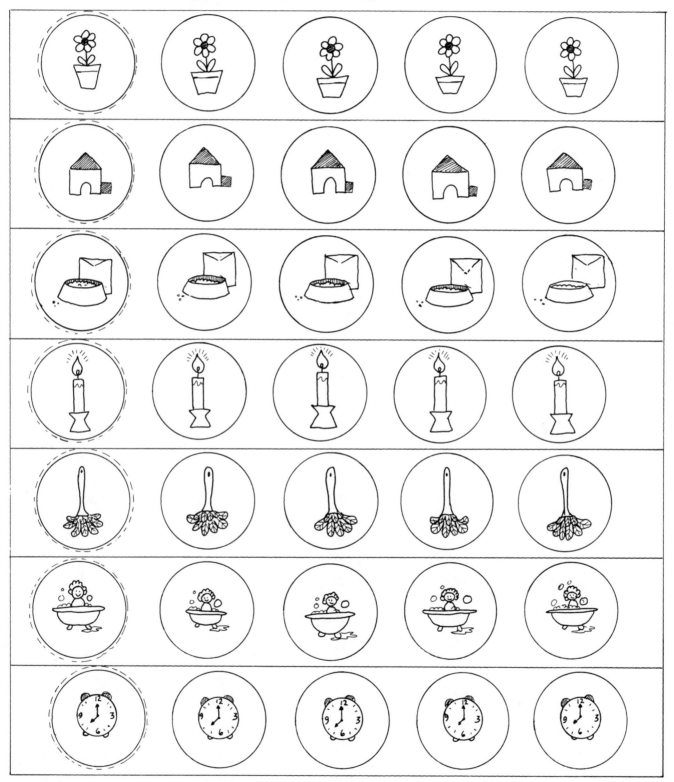

We invite guests to our home. We welcome them and try to make them feel comfortable. This Mitzvah is called HACHNASAT ORCHIM. Here is a house for you to make.

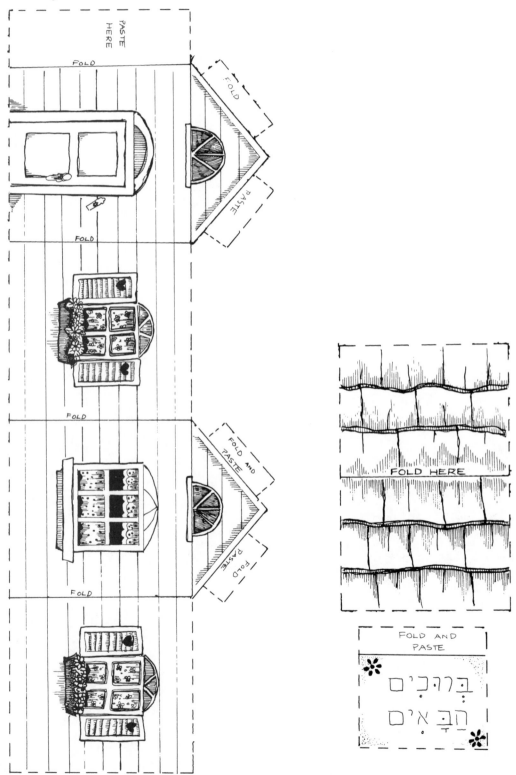

Try to practice the Mitzvah of HACHNASAT ORCHIM. To make your guest feel welcome, fill the plate with special foods. Then color, cut out, and set the table.

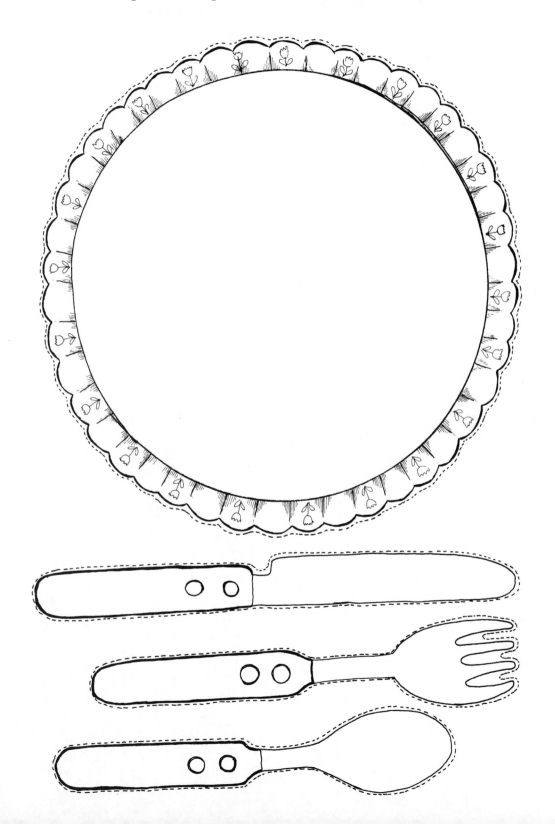

It is a Mitzvah to tell the truth. The Hebrew word for truth is EMET.
Sometimes EMET is hard to tell. Read the story. What should the boy say?

This is your very own Truth Tree. It should remind you always to tell the truth. Can you find the Hebrew letters in the tree? They spell the words EMET. Color the tree.

Choose 4 leaves that show things that are true about you. Remember, some things that are not nice may be true of you. Cut them out and paste them on your Truth Tree. When we see the truth about ourselves, we can try to do better.

Sometimes it is hard to keep your promise. But it is a Mitzvah to keep a promise. In the story, does the girl keep her promise? Make your own promise on the certificate. You can draw or write your promise. Then be sure to keep your word.

TZEDAKAH is an important Mitzvah. TZEDAKAH means doing what is right, like being kind and helping others. One type of TZEDAKAH is helping the poor. We collect our coins in a special container. Color and cut out the labels. Glue them on empty cans. Then you can fill them with coins to give to a special charity.

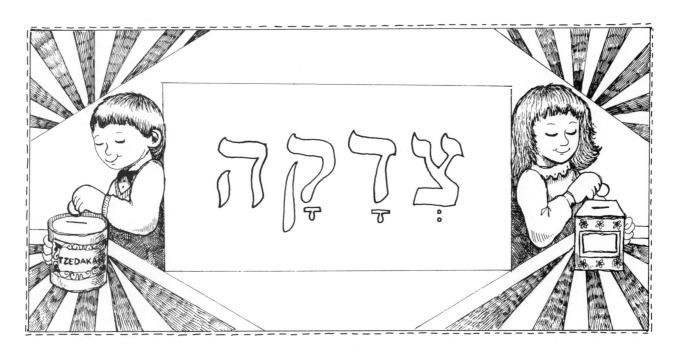

When we visit friends who are sick, we help them to get well again. It is a Mitzvah to visit people who are ill. This commandment is called BIKKUR HOLIM. Sometimes we are not able to visit, but we can still send a get well card. Make the card and cut it out. Send it to someone who is sick.

This is Captain HESED. He is also known as Captain Kindness. HESED means love and kindness. Every day Captain HESED does at least 3 nice things. What nice thing is Captain HESED doing? These acts of kindness are called GEMILUT HASADIM. It is a Mitzvah to do GEMILUT HASADIM. Color the picture.

In what way are all 6 GEMILUT HASADIM alike? Which one is your favorite? Choose 3 GEMILUT HASADIM that you will do. Cut and paste them on the umbrella of Captain HESED. Remember to do your 3 Mitzvot.

GEMILUT HASADIM are kind acts. What kind thing have you done to make someone's life sunnier? Draw or write your answer in the sun. Then color and cut out and wear the badge.

HESED BADGE

What should you do if you find something that does not belong to you? You should try to find the person who lost it. It is a Mitzvah to return lost property. This Mitzvah is called HASHAVAT AVAYDAH. Can you return the lost ball by finding your way through the maze?

Derech is the Hebrew word for "way." *Eretz* is the Hebrew word for "land." DERECH ERETZ means the way we behave to show that we care about other people. When you follow the rules of DERECH ERETZ, you call people by name when you talk to them. You respect people who are older. You are a polite guest when you visit. You dress nicely and keep yourself clean. Here are 2 puppets to make. Can you make them follow the rules of DERECH ERETZ?

It is important to say good things about others. When we say bad things about people, then we are doing LESHON HARAH. LESHON HARAH is something we should not do. Here is a telephone for you to make. Attach the cord to your telephone and call a friend. Practice talking nicely.

TZA'AR BA-ALEY HAYIM means being kind to animals. God created both people and animals. Being kind to animals is a Mitzvah. The Bible tells us the story of Noah and the ark. Noah built the ark and filled it with animals. Here is an ark for you to make. Then you can fill it with the animals on the next page.

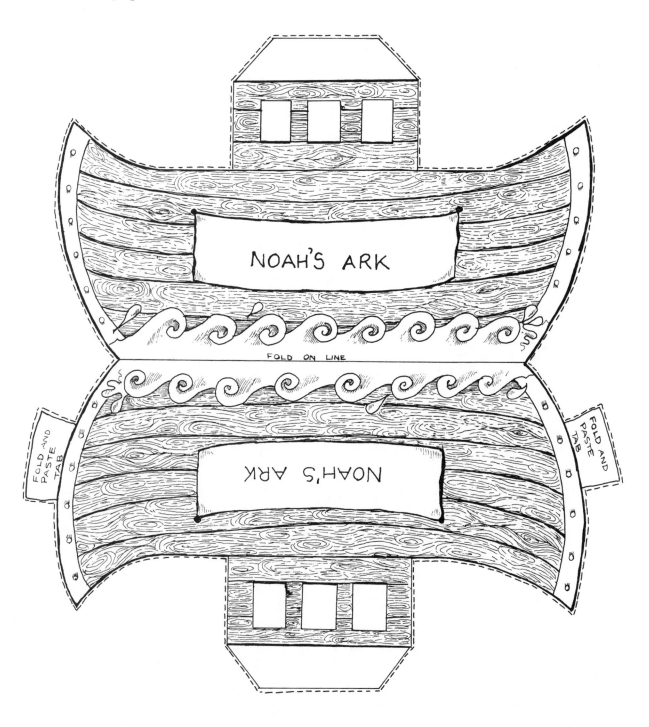

Color, cut, and fold the animals. Then put them in the ark.
What does the story of Noah's ark teach us about taking
care of animals?

AHAVAT YISRAEL is the love that the Jewish people feel for one another. It is also taking care of one another. Draw, color, and cut out the people on this page and on the next page, too. Then paste their hands together. Join your people to your friend's people to make a long chain. This long chain shows that all Jews are connected.

Some people are forced to live where they do not want to live. They are made to do things they do not want to do. It is a Mitzvah to help make them free. This Mitzvah is called PIDYON SHEVUYIM. Jews in Russia are not free to pray and study. One way to practice PIDYON SHEVUYIM is to write letters to people who can help. Your teacher will help you write and mail the letter below.

שָׁלוֹם

Dear _____

Being a good person helps make the world a better place. When we do Mitzvot, we make the world complete. This is called TIKUN OLAM. It means to repair the world. To make the world, use the pieces on this page and on the next two pages. Color and cut out the pieces. See if you can fit them together. Then paste the pieces together on a piece of cardboard.

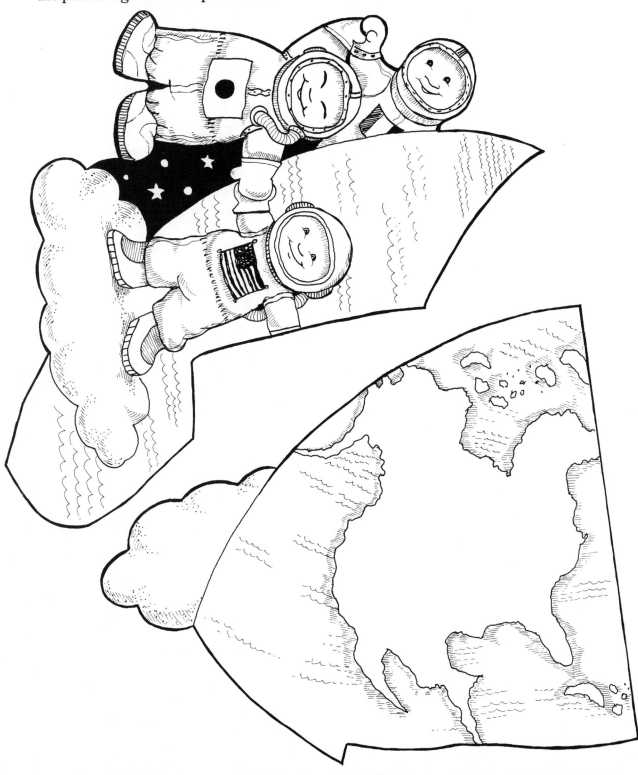

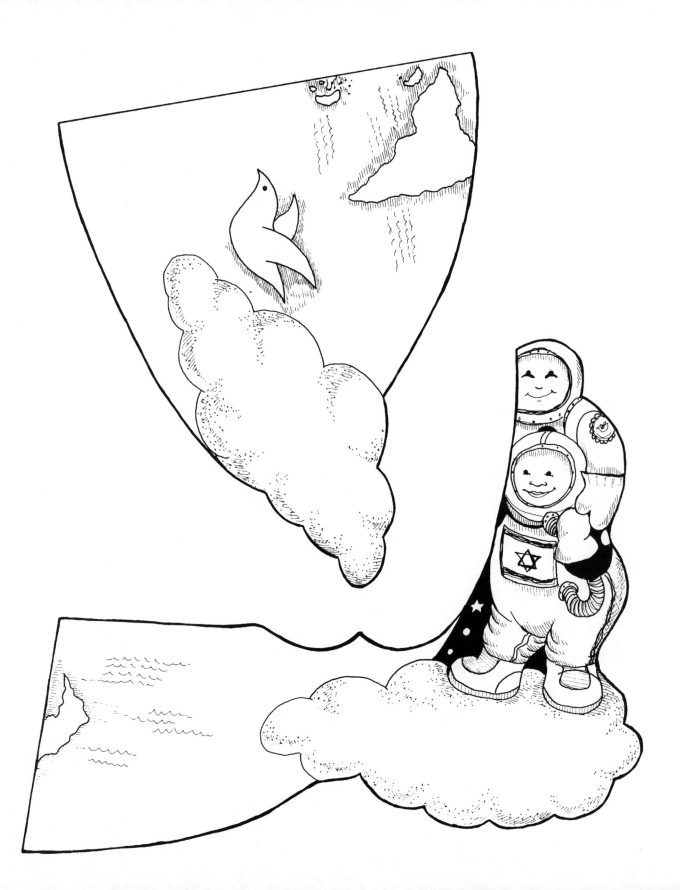

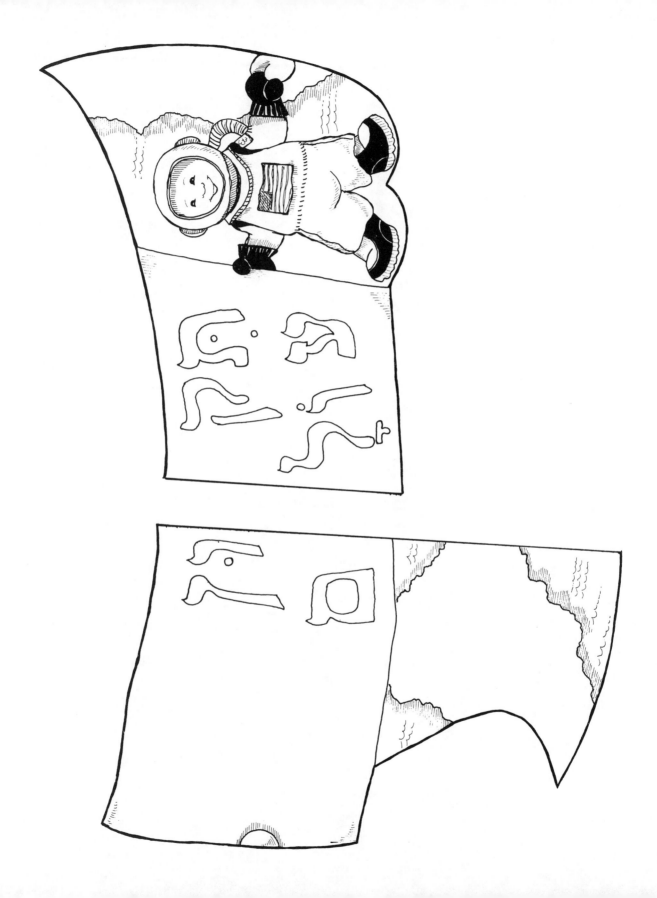

When we do Mitzvot, we get a SHEM TOV—a Good Name. The crown of a good name is even better than the crown of a king. Here is your crown. Color, cut out, and attach the 2 strips to the sides to make the crown. This is the crown of a SHEM TOV for you to wear.

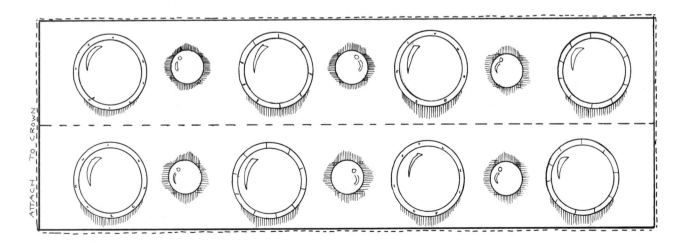

Each picture on the game board should remind you of a Mitzvah you can do.
Cut out the hearts on the next page. Then match the words with the pictures.